THE ULTIMATE
vegan breakfast
BOOK

THE ULTIMATE

vegan breakfast

BOOK

80 MOUTHWATERING PLANT-BASED RECIPES
YOU'LL WANT TO WAKE UP FOR

NADINE HORN & JÖRG MAYER

THE EXPERIMENT

NEW YORK

THE ULTIMATE VEGAN BREAKFAST BOOK: *80 Mouthwatering Plant-Based Recipes You'll Want to Wake Up For*
Text and photography copyright © 2016 by Nadine Horn and Jörg Mayer
Illustrations copyright © 2016 by Nessa Horn
Translation copyright © 2018 The Experiment, LLC

Originally published in Germany as *Vegan Frühstücken Kann Jeder* by Neun Zehn Verlag in 2016.
First published in North America by The Experiment, LLC, in 2018.

The Experiment, LLC | 220 East 23rd Street, Suite 600 | New York, NY 10010-4658
theexperimentpublishing.com

This book contains the opinions and ideas of its authors. It is intended to provide helpful and informative material on the subjects addressed in the book. It is sold with the understanding that the authors and publisher are not engaged in rendering medical, health, or any other kind of personal professional services in the book. The authors and publisher specifically disclaim all responsibility for any liability, loss, or risk—personal or otherwise—that is incurred as a consequence, directly or indirectly, of the use and application of any of the contents of this book.

Many of the designations used by manufacturers and sellers to distinguish their products are claimed as trademarks. Where those designations appear in this book and The Experiment was aware of a trademark claim, the designations have been capitalized.

The Experiment's books are available at special discounts when purchased in bulk for premiums and sales promotions as well as for fund-raising or educational use. For details, contact us at info@theexperimentpublishing.com.

Library of Congress Cataloging-in-Publication Data

Names: Horn, Nadine, author. | Mayer, Jörg, author. | Weiss, Luisa,
  translator.
Title: The ultimate vegan breakfast book : 80 mouthwatering plant-based
  recipes you'll want to wake up for / Nadine Horn and Jörg Mayer ;
  translation by Luisa Weiss.
Other titles: Vegan fruhstucken kahn jeder. English
Description: New York : Experiment, [2018] | Includes index. | "Originally
  published in Germany as Vegan Fruhstucken Kahn Jeder by Neun Zehn Verlag
  in 2016."
Identifiers: LCCN 2018028439 (print) | LCCN 2018035804 (ebook) | ISBN
  9781615195152 (ebook) | ISBN 9781615194889 (pbk.)
Subjects: LCSH: Vegan cooking. | Breakfasts. | LCGFT: Cookbooks.
Classification: LCC TX833 (ebook) | LCC TX833 .H6713 2018 (print) | DDC
  641.5/6362--dc23
LC record available at https://lccn.loc.gov/2018028439

ISBN 978-1-61519-488-9
Ebook ISBN 978-1-61519-515-2

Translation by Luisa Weiss
Manufactured in China

First printing October 2018
10 9 8 7 6 5 4 3 2 1

Dear Readers,

We're happy to share our second cookbook with you, *The Ultimate Vegan Breakfast Book*.

The fact that we published our second cookbook just a year after our first is certainly thanks to the ever-present popularity of vegan cooking, which we've followed with great joy. It's wonderful to see how interest in the subject matter continues to grow organically, and how prejudices against vegans that were prevalent even just a few years ago continue to fall away.

A growing interest in and awareness of the importance of good-quality ingredients and nutrition means that healthy cooking continues to be an important trend in the food world. It's one we've been happy to explore.

Not that our previous recipes were unhealthy. But over the past year we've experimented with many new ingredients, found them to be delicious, and incorporated them into our meal plans. Especially at breakfast time, it's so important to strengthen your body for the day with nutritious and healthy dishes. It doesn't matter what your morning has in store—whether you're working out or going to sit at an office desk—a good and balanced breakfast forms the basis of a good mood, and a great day.

That's how the idea of this cookbook was born. We hope it helps you bring creativity and variety to your breakfast table. Whether it's for a sweet or savory craving, or for big or small appetites, every taste is catered to.

We took care to develop quick and easy recipes as well as longer ones for a lazy weekend brunch. Have fun with *The Ultimate Vegan Breakfast Book*—and eat well!

Nadine & Jörg

CONTENTS

RECIPES

SMOOTHIES, JUICES & CO.

BREAKFAST TO GO

ONE-BOWL WONDERS

HOT OFF THE STOVE

A Perfect Start to the Day

"Just ten more minutes . . ." Who doesn't know that refrain? You hit snooze on the alarm clock, snuggle up in your cozy blanket, and secretly hope that while you're snoozing the clock magically breaks and you're not prevented from finally sleeping in—again.

Even if you're naturally a morning person, accustomed to jumping out of bed bright-eyed and bushy-tailed, mornings are probably still pretty rushed. Between preparing yourself and your family for the day *and* the daily commute, there's often no time for a well-balanced breakfast. But in Germany, we believe that breakfast is the most important meal of the day. It gives you strength and power for the whole day.

So here are some tips for you to take individually or in combination to help you get a good breakfast on the table every morning.

1. PREPARATION IS EVERYTHING

After a long day, you probably think you have better things to do than to get ready for the next morning, but we promise you that just a few minutes in the evening invested in your next day's breakfast are worth it. A lot of our breakfast ideas in this book are easily made the evening before. The next morning, your breakfast will be waiting for you in the fridge.

2. WAKE UP EARLIER

We admit this tip isn't exactly creative and it's definitely not sexy. But it's worth a try. A while ago, we experimented by setting our alarm clocks to 6:00 AM instead of 8:00 AM (most "creative" professionals like us prefer starting work later in the morning, but working longer in the evening—who knows who introduced that idea?). It took a few days of adjustment, but our inner clocks now crave those "ungodly" early hours and we really enjoy the added peace and quiet we get in that time. Who doesn't need more time?

3. BE ACTIVE

Nothing is better for your circulation than movement. You don't have to start your day with a twelve-mile run. Even just fifteen minutes of stretching or yoga are enough and do wonders in working out your entire body.

4. READ A BOOK

Of course staying current on the news is important. But the news can often be overwhelming and depressing, not exactly the kind of stuff that starts your day off right. Since you're getting up earlier now, try to read an inspiring, maybe even humorous book before reaching for your phone or tablet to read the morning news. Your mood and your energy levels will thank you.

5. DRINK A LOT OF WATER

Before your first cup of coffee, you should replenish your liquid stores. Your body loses moisture during sleep, so it doesn't operate on full capacity until you give it back what it lost. One or two glasses of water can work wonders. You can pump that water full of vitamins and minerals, like with our Detox Lemonade on page 31. The fresh citrus juices will get you moving in the morning, we promise.

6. DRINK TEA INSTEAD OF COFFEE

Coffee is not forbidden. Jörg could never give it up—see page 16. But why not try moving your first cup to the late morning instead of first thing? The high caffeine levels of coffee can easily overstimulate your system, and the natural acid in coffee beans isn't exactly the greatest thing you can do to your tummy after a restful sleep.

Nuts, Berries & Seeds

To list every nut, berry, and seed on earth would be beyond the scope of this book. But we'd still love to give you a quick overview of our favorite and most frequently used of these healthy gems. These not only taste delicious but are bursting with fantastic nutritional compounds that do your body good, especially in the morning.

ALMONDS

Almonds are a great source of protein and healthy fats. The nutmeat delivers important B vitamins, beta-carotene, calcium, zinc, and selenium. The brown skin encasing the nut is full of fiber.

CASHEWS

Cashews aren't technically nuts but rather belong to the family of seeds of stone fruits. Compared to other nuts, they are relatively low in fat; they deliver a lot of protein and magnesium.

RASPBERRIES

Raspberries contain a lot of vitamin C, iron, folic acid, magnesium, and potassium. Starting in the twelfth century, they were cultivated in cloister gardens, which makes them one of the oldest cultivated fruits in Europe.

BLUEBERRIES

Fresh blueberries are full of B vitamins and, like raspberries, are a great source of vitamin C. They've also been cultivated for many centuries in Europe.

GOJI BERRIES

These red berries from China are very high in nutrients. They contain more vitamin C than most citrus fruits and are also high in amino acids, B vitamins, minerals, and important trace elements.

FLAXSEED

The best way to consume this nutritional powerhouse is ground, since its healthy oils are better absorbed by the human body once the seeds have been processed. Flaxseed is full of fiber, iron, and calcium, and is a great source of vitamin E.

HEMP SEEDS

Hemp seeds are one of the best sources of omega-3 fatty acids in the world. High in protein, hemp also contains all of the eight essential amino acids that the human body can't produce itself.

CHIA SEEDS

These high-protein seeds were considered an important source of nutrition by the Maya people. They contain a large amount of calcium and iron, deliver long-lasting energy, and help regulate digestion.

SESAME SEEDS

These tiny seeds are a great source of protein and contain a lot of B vitamins and vitamin A. They're also high in fiber and provide the body with high-quality fats.

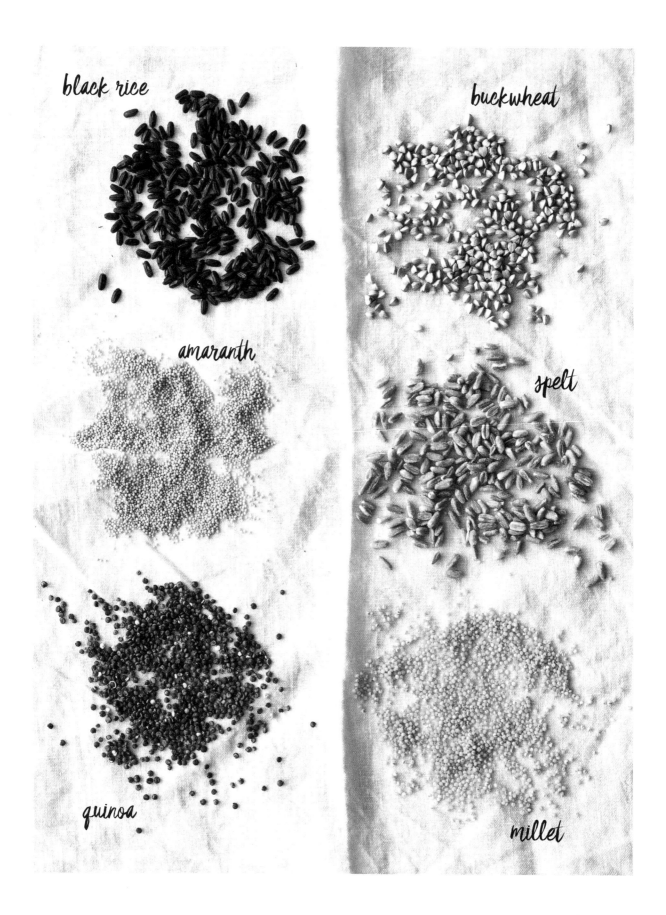

Grains & Cereals

Whether they show up whole, finely ground, or pressed into flakes, grains belong in mueslis and porridges and on every "healthy" breakfast table. Store-bought mixes are often too high in added sugars to be considered nutritious, despite the healthful aspects of the remaining ingredients. Here we introduce you to some of our favorite grains and cereals, and tell you a little bit about why they're so good for you.

AMARANTH, BUCKWHEAT & QUINOA

Amaranth, buckwheat, and quinoa all belong to the family of what are known as pseudocereals. They are gluten-free and full of protein and important minerals, including lysine and lecithin, making them particularly important for nerves and brain development. Just the thing for busy mornings!

SPELT & RYE

In this book, with one exception, we eschew wheat flour and wheat gluten. Instead we use mostly whole grain spelt flour (for pancakes and other similar items) and rye flour (for bread and rolls). Both grains are more aromatic than regular wheat and have higher levels of protein, vitamins, and fiber.

OATS

In this book, we rely on rolled oats for oatmeal and muesli mixtures. In addition to being an excellent source of protein and complex carbohydrates, oats supply zinc, which promotes a healthy immune system, strong hair, and a clear complexion. By the way, oats are naturally gluten-free, but those with celiac disease should always look for a package that notes the oats were processed in a gluten-free facility to avoid contamination.

MILLET

Millet is one of the most nutritionally dense grains in the world, containing B vitamins and trace elements. With its high-quality protein and complex carbohydrates, it helps give a long-lasting feeling of satiety. Millet is also gluten-free and works well in both sweet and savory breakfast recipes.

BLACK RICE

We have a particular affection for black rice. It's high in protein, antioxidants, and minerals. It's also a great source of iron. Unlike white or brown rice, black rice is sold unhulled, giving it a deliciously nutty aroma. Originally, black rice came from China, but today it is cultivated around the world.

Coffee Love

Jörg, the coffee junkie

There are those, like Nadine, who prefer a cup of tea in the morning. But for the majority of us, coffee is a nonnegotiable part of the morning breakfast routine. Still, there's a lot of information out there on coffee that isn't widely known. It's worth your time to take a few minutes to learn about "black gold," Maybe while sipping your morning mug.

VARIETIES & ORIGINS

Although there are around sixty different kinds of coffee in the world, only two are relevant for the world market: arabica, which makes up 70 percent of world production, and canephora or robusta.

The best coffee-growing regions are near the equator, although arabica plants flourish in the cooler hilly areas, while robusta can sustain higher temperatures in flatter regions such as in Brazil or Vietnam.

Although arabica is considered the finer and more complex of the two coffee types, we generally feel that with coffee—and everything, really—you should drink what you like! Robusta has twice as much caffeine as arabica and tastes earthier and more traditionally like "coffee."

If you suffer from a nervous tummy, you should stay away from darker roasts like espresso, since these are more acidic.

STORAGE

General wisdom decrees that the fresher the coffee is, the longer you can store it without it losing its aroma. But the truth is, as soon as the coffee (whole beans or ground) is exposed to air, it begins to lose aroma. Therefore be sure to store your coffee in airtight containers where it is dry and cool. Many coffee roasters, especially small companies, deliver their beans in resealable bags with built-in vents, which keeps the coffee fresh for a longer amount of time.

PREPARATION METHODS

Using today's very popular pod coffee machines is a much more expensive way of preparing your morning boost, not to mention catastrophic for the environment. There are many more classic techniques that will not only save you money, but also allow you to savor your sip even more in the process of brewing.

Coffee makers that grind *and* brew are great all-purpose tools. They're not easy to clean, though, especially when you take into consideration the recommendation of daily cleaning to avoid mold formation. So perhaps they're not that great, and truthfully, they're not all that good at making coffee either.

An affordable way to make good coffee is a French press. If you like, you can buy a manual coffee grinder and make your own ground coffee fresh every day.

If you've got a classic ceramic (or glass, or plastic) coffee cone filter stashed away in your attic or basement, it's certainly a good option to dig it out and add it to your arsenal. Sometimes simplest is best.

Those who love espresso should rely on making it in stovetop moka pots, the smaller the better. Online you can find lots of great guides and videos to help you understand your espresso pot. Here's a little tip from an Italian former neighbor of ours: Place one to two tablespoons raw sugar on top of the ground coffee before closing up your moka pot for a delicious caramel-flavored espresso.

Passionate coffee drinkers take care of their high-tech espresso machines as if they were soulmates. But you're only going to get real pleasure out of this caliber of machine if you have no problem spending $200 to $600 (or more!) on it and a good coffee grinder.

I personally am a big fan of cold brew coffee, a simple and digestible way of making coffee in which ground beans are soaked in cold water, producing a concentrated coffee that can be kept in the fridge and very easily used in various coffee drinks. If you're curious to know more, turn to page 160.

WHAT TO BUY, AND WHERE?

We recommend buying fair trade coffee or, better yet, coffee directly from the source. This way the coffee farmers get more money for their harvest and you support the local growing and harvesting practices. Most importantly, we feel that it's better to spend a little more on good-quality coffee and less on your coffee maker.

A Note from Jörg: Since I love drinking coffee, but certainly am no expert, I want to give thanks to Heiko from schwarzmahler.de for his help during research. On his site, Heiko sells directly sourced and incredibly delicious coffee, as well as gives detailed information on the growing and harvest practices for each coffee.

ceramic filter

moka pot

French press

manual grinder

Tea Time!

Nadine, the Tea Lady

Jörg may love his coffee, but I'm a true tea lady.

For me, a good start to any day includes a cup of tea. Just the ritual alone—boiling the water, choosing the tea, steeping the leaves—makes me feel relaxed.

I don't drink the same tea every morning. I prefer to choose the tea based on how I'm feeling on any particular day.

Most teas are really healthy and boast a good deal of great nutrients. I think it's important to buy organic loose teas, for both my own health and that of the environment.

LOOSE OR BAGGED TEA?

The biggest difference between loose and bagged tea is in the size and quality of the tea leaves. Packaged in most tea bags is either very finely chopped tea called "fannings" or powdered tea, called "dust." In addition to having higher levels of pesticides, bagged tea often suffers from a lack of flavor and could be polluted with artificial aroma and flavor enhancers.

Loose teas retain far more of their essential oils for longer and are healthier. The generally accepted dictum that loose tea is more expensive than bagged tea isn't true. A tea bag can only be brewed once, but loose tea can be brewed more than once.

I like having both loose and bagged tea at home, since it's hard to argue with the convenience of a tea bag. But in terms of flavor, I far prefer loose tea. It's not just more flavorful, but it's also more environmentally friendly. If you invest in a higher quality tea, you'll taste the difference and won't look back!

Here's a little overview of the most popular kinds of tea you can choose from.

BLACK TEA

Black tea is one of the most commonly consumed kinds of tea. Black tea is the product of the tea plant, *Camellia sinensis*, as are green tea, oolong tea, and white tea. Tea leaves turn black through the oxidation process, which gives black tea its intense, familiar flavor.

Black tea contains caffeine. It may only be half as much as the caffeine in coffee, but it's advisable to not drink caffeine just before going to bed.

The biggest tea planting zones are in India, which is where many black teas also get their names, Assam or Darjeeling, for example.

I like drinking black tea with soy or nut milk, but many enjoy their black tea plain or simply with a slice of lemon.

Flavored teas are also an integral part of the black tea category. The best known and most popular is of course Earl Grey tea, which is perfumed with bergamot oil. It's a typical English breakfast tea and also one of my favorites. My other favorites: Darjeeling and Chai Latte (page 157).

GREEN TEA

Unlike with black tea, no oxidation takes place when green tea is produced. Instead, the leaves are left to wilt, then briefly heated to lock in the essential compounds and prevent oxidation. The oldest and most beloved type of green tea is sencha, which is mostly cultivated in China and Japan. My favorites: jasmine sencha and genmaicha (green tea mixed with roasted rice).

MATCHA

Growing ever more popular, matcha belongs to the green tea category. But the production of matcha is very different and one of the most labor-intensive in the world of tea. The tea plant varietal used for matcha is grown only in Japan on special "shadow tea" plantations. In these conditions, the tea leaves are covered with dark nets four weeks before the harvest. The plants compensate for the sudden lack of sunlight by producing large amounts of chlorophyll to survive. After the leaves are harvested by hand, they are steamed to preserve both the leaf and the delicate compounds within. Finally, the tea leaves are dried and slowly ground in a granite mill, resulting in the fine, shockingly green powder that characterizes matcha.

Once you've understood the painstaking work that goes into producing matcha powder, the accompanying high prices begin to make a lot more sense.

To make a cup of matcha tea, you need a ceramic cup and the *chasen*, a whisk specifically made only for this purpose. I have a lot of fun with the ritual of making matcha. If you find out that you enjoy it too, I highly recommend a visit to a Japanese tea ceremony!

My favorites: plain matcha, Matcha Latte (page 156).

ROOIBOS OR REDBUSH TEA

Rooibos is not actually tea in the classical sense since it's not made from tea leaves. Rooibos comes from

rooibos

black tea

bagged tea

loose tea

matcha

green tea

a broom-like plant native to South Africa, whose branches are cut and subsequently fermented.

What I love about rooibos is that it's completely caffeine-free, but its color and taste are similar to black tea. So it's great for those with sensitive stomachs and for kids.

Rooibos tea contains an array of health-promoting compounds as well as minerals and trace elements. I like drinking it with oat, soy, or almond milk. My favorites: plain rooibos tea with almond milk, and rooibos chai (prepare the Chai Latte on page 157 using rooibos tea instead of black tea).

HERBAL TEAS

Herbal teas like rooibos and fruit-based teas aren't brewed from tea leaves. I consider them to be more like aromatic infusions made from fresh or dried plant elements like leaves, petals, or seeds.

It's really easy to make wonderful herbal teas yourself. Find a good source for loose dried herbs or edible flowers—peppermint, chamomile, elderflower, hibiscus, etc.—and mix your own concoction that makes you feel good. These ingredients make fine caffeine-free drinks, as will fresh mint leaves, or sliced ginger mixed with hot water and a splash of maple syrup.

My favorites: Kamilli Vanilli (page 158), Ginger Tea (page 159), and brewed lemon balm or raspberry leaves.

STORAGE

It's best to decant your teas into metal or ceramic containers with airtight lids, then store them somewhere dark and cool, where they will last for around three years.

Maybe you're as big a tea fan as I am. For everyone else, I hope my overview motivates you to find out more—and perhaps to even begin your own customized tea collection.

Cheers!

Tips & Tricks

KALA NAMAK

Kala namak, also known as black salt or Indian salt, is a volcanic stone salt. Its smell and taste are sulfurous and reminiscent of boiled eggs. When combined with avocado or tofu as an egg substitute, this wonderful salt is a craveable addition to vegan breakfast recipes.

FROZEN SMOOTHIE KITS

We often hear from friends and acquaintances that they'd like to prepare a morning smoothie for themselves, but feel overwhelmed by the amount of time and effort it would require. A great solution is to find a quiet moment in the week to prep and freeze fresh fruits and vegetables in individual portion sizes. Then all you have to do in the morning is dump a portion into your high-speed blender and add some liquid before processing. It's a really quick way to make a nice, creamy smoothie every morning.

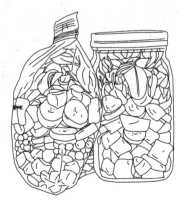

BREAKFASTS AROUND THE WORLD

For breakfast, Germans like to eat rolls with jam or cured meat, along with a cup of coffee or tea. That is, if they're breakfasting at all— because according to statistics, most Germans don't eat breakfast! The English love their porridge and a cup of Earl Grey tea in the morning, but on Sundays like to indulge in a "full English" (page 153). The French want nothing more than a café au lait and a fresh croissant; even if it's late morning, it's always called *petit dejeuner*. In America, the beloved pancake features widely, even if on busy weekdays many choose corn flakes or other prepackaged cereals. In Asia, however, the typical "sweet" breakfast of the Western world is unheard of. Instead, savory soups and dim sum are typical choices. In Japan, it could be miso soup, rice, and *natto* (fermented soybeans). In India and Africa, the day usually starts with something savory, like fried bread or pancakes with vegetables.

No matter where you're from or in which direction your personal taste veers, we've done our best to offer something that fits everyone. Sweet or savory, hearty or light—try them all, and maybe you'll even find a new way to enjoy breakfast!

WHY NO NUTRITIONAL INFORMATION?

While we were doing research on the nutritional information for each recipe in this book, we found that the basic caloric calculations of ingredients were fundamentally wrong. Until recently, the caloric value of food items was calculated by burning the item and measuring the energy thereby produced. This method is more than one hundred years old, and has been shown through recent research to not be accurate.

A new methodology has yet to be developed, but generally speaking, the assumption is that highly processed foods have higher calories than unprocessed foods. For this reason, we decided not to label our recipes with typical nutrition stats, but simply identify them as "light," "balanced," or "comfort food."

A NOTE ON THE RECIPES

We assume that even if not labeled as such, only vegan ingredients will be used in our recipes (like vegan margarine, etc.). We have also designated a recipe as gluten-free even if it includes rolled oats or soy sauce; we assume that those with celiac disease will be sure to purchase the gluten-free versions of these staple ingredients. Finally, in this book, sugar-free means free of refined sugar, rather than free of natural sugars (like those in fruits and dates).

Recipes

SMOOTHIES, JUICES & CO.

Avocado Super Smoothie 27

Pomegranate Smoothie 29

Detox Lemonade 31

Hemp & Date Smoothie 33

"Buttermilk" Shake 35

The Green Classic 37

Tropical Energy 39

Super Antioxidant Shake 41

Pear Oat Shake 43

Pineapple Carrot Smoothie 45

Strawberry Chia Smoothie 47

Infused Water 49
Cucumber & Mint
Grapefruit & Rosemary
Strawberry & Mint

Turmeric Tonic 51

Beets & Berries 53

AVOCADO SUPER SMOOTHIE
WITH COCONUT WATER AND BLUEBERRIES

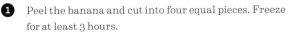

Preparation time 5 minutes • **Freezing time** 3 hours • **Makes** 2 smoothies

light

We love coconut water! Just as much as we love avocados and blueberries, especially at breakfast time. The good fat in avocados helps your body absorb the great nutritional elements in the other ingredients.

1 banana

½ ripe avocado

1⅔ cups (50 g) spinach or 2½ cups (50 g) washed, stemmed, and torn curly kale

¾ cup (200 ml) almond milk

½ cup (100 ml) coconut water

1 handful fresh blueberries

(GLUTEN FREE) (SUGAR FREE) (SOY FREE)

1 Peel the banana and cut into four equal pieces. Freeze for at least 3 hours.

2 Peel and pit the avocado (see Tip). Cut into pieces.

3 Place the banana, avocado, leafy greens, almond milk, coconut water, and blueberries in a food processor or high-speed blender and process until smooth.

4 Pour into two glasses and serve immediately.

TIP

If you leave the avocado pit in the remaining half of the fruit, you can store the avocado in the fridge for up to a day without it turning brown.

POMEGRANATE SMOOTHIE

SWEET, SOUR, AND REFRESHING

Preparation time 10 minutes • **Freezing time** 3 hours • **Makes** 2 smoothies

You have to use a little elbow grease to get out all the delicious seeds from a pomegranate. But we have a tip to make it easier, pinky-swear! In any case, the effort is worth it, because pomegranates are full of vitamins to prepare you for the day ahead.

1 banana

2 handfuls fresh or frozen raspberries

1 ⅔ cups (400 ml) orange juice

Seeds from 1 pomegranate (see Tip)

1 Peel the banana and cut into four equal pieces. Freeze for at least 3 hours.

2 Place the banana, raspberries, orange juice, and pomegranate seeds (reserving a few seeds for garnish) in a food processor or high-speed blender and process until smooth.

3 Pour into two glasses and serve immediately, topped with a few pomegranate seeds.

GLUTEN FREE · SUGAR FREE · SOY FREE

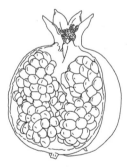

TIP

It's easiest to remove pomegranate seeds by cutting the fruit in half, submerging the halves in a bowl of cold water, then peeling back the skin. Be careful not to squish the seeds too much so their delicious flavor is preserved.

DETOX LEMONADE
VITAMIN-PACKED REFRESHMENT

Preparation time 5 minutes • **Makes** 2 drinks

Our Detox Lemonade is perfect to help replenish your fluids first thing in the morning. In addition, it packs enough vitamin C to keep you safe from colds in the autumn and winter months.

1 lemon

2 tangerines

1 tablespoon coconut sugar

Ice cubes

1 Juice the lemon. Peel the tangerines, discard the skins, and separate into sections.

2 Place the lemon juice, tangerines, coconut sugar, and 2 cups (500 ml) cold water in a food processor or high-speed blender and process until smooth.

3 Place ice cubes in two glasses and divide the lemonade between them. Serve immediately.

GLUTEN FREE   SOY FREE

TIP

Detox Lemonade can be enjoyed either cold or hot. In the winter, simply replace the cold water with hot water for a warming morning treat.

HEMP & DATE SMOOTHIE

CREAMY AND ENERGIZING

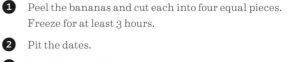

Preparation time 5 minutes • **Freezing time** 3 hours • **Makes** 2 smoothies

Hemp seeds are full of vitamins and minerals, and the natural sugar in dates will give you a great kick of energy for your day.

2 bananas

8 dried Medjool dates or 10 regular dates

1 vanilla bean

2 tablespoons hemp seeds

2½ cups (600 ml) almond milk

1½ teaspoons ground cinnamon

1 Peel the bananas and cut each into four equal pieces. Freeze for at least 3 hours.

2 Pit the dates.

3 Split the vanilla bean open lengthwise and scrape out the seeds with a knife. Set aside the pod.

4 Place the bananas, dates, vanilla seeds, hemp seeds, almond milk, and cinnamon in a food processor or high-speed blender and process until smooth.

5 Pour into two glasses and serve immediately.

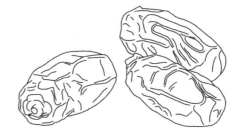

TIP

This smoothie also doubles as a perfect sports drink, reviving you after any workout.

"BUTTERMILK" SHAKE

WITH ORANGE AND ALMOND

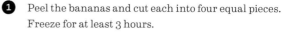

Preparation time 5 minutes • **Freezing time** 3 hours • **Makes** 2 shakes

The sweet-sour mixture of almond milk and freshly juiced oranges immediately made us think of buttermilk. The frozen banana makes the whole thing wonderfully creamy and gives you sustained nutrition for the day.

2 bananas

2 medium oranges

¾ cup (200 ml) almond milk (see Tip)

① Peel the bananas and cut each into four equal pieces. Freeze for at least 3 hours.

② Grate the zest of the oranges until you have 1 tablespoon. Juice the oranges, straining out the seeds.

③ Place the banana, orange zest, orange juice, and almond milk in a food processor or high-speed blender and process until smooth.

④ Pour into two glasses and serve immediately.

GLUTEN FREE   SUGAR FREE   SOY FREE

TIP

You can make this shake with any other plant-based milk. We think cashew milk is also a great choice here.

THE GREEN CLASSIC
OUR FAVORITE WAY TO DRINK OUR GREENS

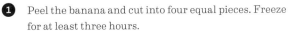

Preparation time 10 minutes • **Freezing time** 3 hours • **Makes** 2 smoothies

light

Green smoothies are everywhere! There are a million ways to make them, and we love experimenting with new ingredients, like wild herbs. But our all-time favorite is this one, with spicy spinach and parsley to balance the sweet fruits.

1 banana

1 orange

1 kiwi (see Tips)

1 handful baby spinach

3 sprigs fresh flat-leaf parsley

(GLUTEN FREE) (SUGAR FREE) (SOY FREE)

1 Peel the banana and cut into four equal pieces. Freeze for at least three hours.

2 Peel the orange and discard the skin. Separate the orange into segments. Cut off the woody base of the kiwi and then slice into pieces.

3 Place the banana, orange, kiwi, spinach, parsley, and 1 cup (250 ml) cold water in a food processor or high-speed blender and process until smooth.

4 Pour into two glasses and serve immediately.

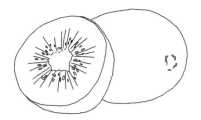

TIPS

You don't need to peel organic kiwis; just give them a good rinse. The skins will naturally break up in the blender.

You can slowly figure out your favorite smoothie flavor combinations. If you have a great source of fresh wild herbs, such as sorrel or nettles, try adding some to this smoothie. You can also keep herbs on hand all year by freezing fresh-picked leaves.

TROPICAL ENERGY

WITH GRAPEFRUIT AND COCONUT

Preparation time 5 minutes • **Makes** 2 drinks

Coconut water is the fresh juice of unripe green coconuts, and should not be confused with coconut milk. It has a remarkably high concentration of nutrients and is just the right thing to help you face whatever challenges the day brings.

1 grapefruit (see Tip)

1 lemon

1 lime

¾ cup (200 ml) coconut water

1 tablespoon agave syrup

Ice cubes

1 Juice the grapefruit, lemon, and lime. Discard the remaining pulp and skins.

2 Place the citrus juices, coconut water, and agave syrup in a food processor or high-speed blender and process until smooth.

3 Place ice cubes in two glasses and divide the drink between them. Serve immediately.

TIP

If you don't like the bitter grapefruit flavor, replace it with two oranges or two tangerines.

SUPER ANTIOXIDANT SHAKE

WITH BLUEBERRIES AND GOJI BERRIES

light

Preparation time 5 minutes • **Chilling time** 5 minutes • **Makes** 2 shakes

The antioxidant chemical compounds called anthocyanins that give blueberries their dark blue color also help your body relieve stress, and neutralize free radicals.

½ cup (70 g) fresh or frozen blueberries

2 cups (500 ml) almond milk

2½ tablespoons ground flaxseed

1½ tablespoons maple syrup

2 tablespoons goji berries

2 tablespoons chia seeds

1 Place the blueberries, almond milk, flaxseed, and maple syrup in a food processor or high-speed blender and process until smooth.

2 Divide between two glasses and top with the goji berries and chia seeds. Place in the fridge for 5 minutes for the chia to swell before serving.

TIP

If you have a source for wild blueberries in the summer, buy or pick extra and freeze them for the winter months. Blueberries maintain their essential nutrients even when frozen.

PEAR OAT SHAKE
DRINKABLE MUESLI

light

Preparation time 5 minutes • **Makes** 2 shakes

Our Pear Oat Shake is more filling than regular smoothies, thanks to the oats, flaxseed, and hemp seeds. It will definitely tide you over until lunch.

1 pear (see Tip)

¼ cup (20 g) rolled oats

1 tablespoon hemp seeds

1 tablespoon ground flaxseed

1½ teaspoons almond butter

1½ teaspoons ground cardamom

½ teaspoon ground cinnamon

1⅔ cups (400 ml) almond milk (see Tip)

Ice cubes

Crushed pistachios (optional)

Toasted unsweetened shredded coconut (optional)

1 Halve and core the pear, keeping the skin on. Cut into pieces.

2 Place the pear, oats, hemp seeds, flaxseed, almond butter, cardamom, cinnamon, and almond milk in a food processor or high-speed blender and process until smooth.

3 Place ice cubes in two glasses and divide the shake between them. Top with pistachios and coconut, if you choose. Serve immediately.

(GLUTEN FREE) (SUGAR FREE) (SOY FREE)

TIP

The pear can easily be replaced with a sweet variety of apple. Adjust the amount of almond milk you use for a thicker or thinner shake.

PINEAPPLE CARROT SMOOTHIE

EXOTICALLY WARMING WAKE-UP CALL

light

Preparation time 5 minutes • **Makes** 2 smoothies

The flaxseed oil in this smoothie helps your body process the fat-soluble vitamins in the carrots. Pineapple and warming ginger give the smoothie a fresh and fruity flavor that will definitely help wake you up.

2 medium carrots (5 ounces/150 g total)

½-inch (1 cm) piece fresh ginger

1¼ cups (200 g) fresh pineapple chunks

Juice of ½ lemon

¼ teaspoon flaxseed oil

1 Wash and peel the carrots. Cut into pieces.

2 Peel and slice the ginger.

3 Place the carrots, ginger, pineapple, lemon juice, and 1¼ cups (300 ml) cold water in a food processor or high-speed blender and process until smooth.

4 Pour into two glasses and drizzle each drink with flaxseed oil. Serve immediately.

GLUTEN FREE   SUGAR FREE   SOY FREE

TIP

Freeze chunks of ripe, juicy pineapple to always have what you need for a nicely chilled smoothie on hand.

STRAWBERRY CHIA SMOOTHIE

PACKS A PINK PUNCH

Preparation time 5 minutes • **Chilling time** 5 minutes • **Makes** 2 smoothies

Chia seeds contain a lot of great nutrients, including protein and more calcium than dairy milk! It's no wonder that in the original Mayan language, chia *means "strength"—all the more reason to enjoy them at breakfast.*

12 strawberries

1½ tablespoons ground flaxseed

2 cups (500 ml) soy milk

1½ teaspoons maple syrup

1½ tablespoons chia seeds

1 Wash, dry, and hull the strawberries.

2 Place the strawberries, flaxseed, soy milk, and maple syrup in a food processor or high-speed blender and process until smooth.

3 Pour into two glasses, divide the chia seeds between them, and stir. Place in the fridge for 5 minutes for the chia to swell before serving.

TIP

Chia seeds can keep for a long time in a dry, dark spot—up to five years. We don't think they'll last that long, though, with all the ways you can enjoy them at breakfast and beyond!

INFUSED WATER

SAY GOODBYE TO PLAIN, BORING WATER!

Preparation time 5 minutes • **Chilling time** 8 hours • **Makes** 2 servings each

Drinking a big glass of water first thing in the morning helps kickstart your digestive system. If plain water is too boring for you, try infusing it with fruits and herbs—there's no limit to what ingredients you can combine! Simply add your ingredients to a pitcher of water, let sit overnight in the fridge, then enjoy over ice. It's really easy, looks beautiful, and is fun to prepare, too.

CUCUMBER & MINT

4 cucumber slices

3 lime slices

3 sprigs fresh mint

1. Combine the ingredients in a pitcher with 2 cups (500 ml) water. Cover and refrigerate overnight (8 hours).

2. To serve, strain over ice into tall glasses.

GRAPEFRUIT & ROSEMARY

2 grapefruit slices

2 sprigs fresh rosemary

STRAWBERRY & MINT

3 strawberries, halved

2 sprigs fresh mint

TURMERIC TONIC

THE POWER ELIXIR

light

Preparation time 5 minutes • **Makes** 2 drinks

Packed with superfoods, this tonic is a real magic potion for us. Turmeric and ginger are some of the healthiest items in our pantry, and we can't imagine our recipes without them.

1-inch (2.5 cm) piece fresh turmeric

1-inch (2.5 cm) piece fresh ginger

¾ cup (200 ml) coconut water

¾ cup (200 ml) fresh orange juice

Juice of 1 lemon

2 teaspoons maple syrup

Pinch of salt

Ice cubes

GLUTEN FREE SOY FREE

1 Peel the turmeric and ginger. Place them with the coconut water in a blender and process until as smooth as possible.

2 Pour through a fine-mesh sieve into a pitcher. Stir in the orange and lemon juices, maple syrup, and salt.

3 Place ice cubes in two glasses and divide the tonic between them. Serve immediately.

TIP

If you can't find fresh turmeric, substitute 1½ teaspoons ground turmeric.

BEETS & BERRIES

THE GOOD-MOOD SMOOTHIE

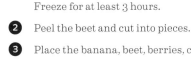

Preparation time 5 minutes • **Freezing time** 3 hours • **Makes** 2 smoothies

Beets contain mood-boosting elements and are a great ingredient for a good start to the day. Combined with the vitamins from red berries, there's nothing much that can go wrong here.

½ banana

1 medium raw red beet (2¾ ounces/80 g, see Tip)

⅔ cup (100 g) fresh or frozen red berries (any kind)

1 tablespoon Cashew Butter (page 177)

1 teaspoon ground flaxseed

¾ cup (200 ml) Cashew Milk (page 185)

1 Peel the banana and cut into two equal pieces. Freeze for at least 3 hours.

2 Peel the beet and cut into pieces.

3 Place the banana, beet, berries, cashew butter, flaxseed, and cashew milk in a food processor or high-speed blender and process until smooth.

4 Pour into two glasses and serve immediately.

TIP

If you can get beets with the greens still attached, use the leaves in this smoothie, too. They contain even more nutrients than the root. Wash them and tear into pieces first.

BREAKFAST TO GO

SWEDISH BAGEL

WITH CREAM CHEESE, DILL, AND BEETS

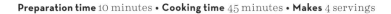

Preparation time 10 minutes • **Cooking time** 45 minutes • **Makes** 4 servings

comfort food

At first glance, Nordic cuisine doesn't seem particularly vegan-friendly. But luckily it's easy to creatively reimagine many classic Nordic recipes, like this bagel topped with sweet sliced beets and homemade cashew cream cheese. Bye-bye lox and schmear!

1 large beet (5 ounces/150 g)

4 bagels, any variety

6 tablespoons Cashew Cream Cheese (page 179)

1 tablespoon minced fresh chives

2 tablespoons fresh dill

1. Wash the beet, place in a pot, and cover with water. Cover the pot with a lid and bring to a boil. Simmer for 40 to 45 minutes, until the beet is fork-tender.

2. Drain the beet and let cool to room temperature.

3. Peel the beet and cut into ¼ -inch-thick (5 mm) round slices.

4. Slice each bagel in half and toast in a toaster or dry nonstick skillet, cut sides down, for 2 minutes.

5. Spread one side of a bagel with 1½ tablespoons of the cream cheese. Arrange one quarter of the beet slices on the cream cheese and garnish with the chives and dill. Top with the remaining bagel half. Repeat with the remaining bagels and fillings. Serve.

TIP

If you can find cooked beets in your supermarket, those are fine to use. Pickled red beets taste great here, too.

OVERNIGHT BUCKWHEAT PORRIDGE

LAYERED TO GO

Preparation time 15 minutes • **Soaking time** 8 hours • **Makes** 2 servings

In this recipe, soaked buckwheat groats are pureed with fresh berries, then combined with sweet fruit and fresh yogurt. Pour your nutritious and tasty breakfast into a jam jar and take it with you to work or school.

½ cup (80 g) buckwheat groats

4 fresh or frozen strawberries

1 handful fresh or frozen raspberries

2 teaspoons maple syrup

FOR THE ASSEMBLY

⅔ cup (175 g) plain soy yogurt

½ banana, sliced

2 fresh strawberries, halved

1 handful fresh blueberries

6 tablespoons Granola (page 183)

 Mix the buckwheat groats and 1 cup (240 ml) water in a small bowl. Cover and refrigerate overnight (8 hours).

❷ The next morning, drain and rinse the buckwheat in a strainer until the water runs clean. Place in a food processor or high-speed blender with the strawberries, raspberries, and maple syrup and process until smooth.

❸ To assemble, divide the buckwheat porridge between two jam jars (or bowls, if you're eating in). Spoon the yogurt evenly over both.

❹ Top each portion with the banana, fresh strawberries, blueberries, and granola.

TIP

We think it's easiest to enjoy this porridge on the go in a jelly or jam jar with a screw top. We like to save nice, big jars precisely for this purpose. Just remove the labels beforehand.

OAT & CRANBERRY COOKIES

FOR DUNKING IN MILK — OR COFFEE — ANY TIME OF DAY

Preparation time 15 minutes • Baking time 15 minutes • **Makes** 10 cookies

Don't have time for a bowl and spoon? Try eating your morning granola in cookie form! The banana keeps these breakfast cookies moist. They're best enjoyed with a big glass of soy or nut milk.

¼ cup (30 g) raw almonds

1 tablespoon hemp seeds

1 ripe banana

1 cup (90 g) rolled oats

⅓ cup (30 g) unsweetened shredded coconut

Pinch of salt

½ teaspoon ground cinnamon

2 tablespoons unsweetened dried cranberries (see Tip)

1 tablespoon ground flaxseed

2 tablespoons coconut oil, melted

1 teaspoon maple syrup

1. Preheat the oven to 350°F (180°C). Line a baking sheet with parchment paper.

2. Finely chop the almonds. Crush the hemp seeds with a mortar and pestle. Peel the banana and mash with a fork in a large bowl.

3. Add the almonds, hemp seeds, oats, coconut, salt, cinnamon, cranberries, flaxseed, coconut oil, and maple syrup to the bowl and stir, until the dough holds together.

4. Divide the dough into ten equal portions (about 2 tablespoons each) and place on the prepared baking sheet, spacing them about 2 inches (5 cm) apart to allow for spread. Bake for 15 minutes, or until golden brown.

5. Let cool completely on a wire rack. Store in an airtight container for up to 4 weeks.

TIP

Try this cookie with diced dried apricots or pineapple instead of cranberries. Or use dairy-free chocolate chips for an even sweeter variation.

BREAKFAST BURRITO
WITH MUSHROOMS AND CHICKPEA "SCRAMBLE"

Preparation time 25 minutes • **Makes** 4 burritos

Everyone loves a breakfast burrito—they're delicious and pretty practical. Prepare your chickpea "scramble" in the evening and then on busy mornings just pack a burrito in your lunch box. You'll garner envious looks from your coworkers.

FOR THE MUSHROOM TOPPING

2 tablespoons olive oil

10 white or cremini mushrooms, sliced

1 teaspoon salt

FOR THE CHICKPEA "SCRAMBLE"

2 cups (200 g) chickpea flour

¼ cup (20 g) rolled oats

½ teaspoon ground turmeric

½ teaspoon ground paprika

½ teaspoon freshly ground black pepper

1 tablespoon olive oil

FOR THE BURRITOS

4 whole wheat tortillas

2 tomatoes

1 avocado, peeled and pitted

2 teaspoons kala namak (see Tip)

1 To make the mushroom topping, pour the olive oil into a nonstick skillet over high heat. When the oil is hot, sauté the mushrooms until golden brown, 5 to 7 minutes, and season with the salt. Scrape the mushrooms onto a dish and set aside.

2 To make the chickpea "scramble," whisk together the chickpea flour, oats, turmeric, paprika, and pepper in a medium bowl. Whisk in 1 cup (240 ml) water until smooth.

3 Pour the olive oil into the pan used for the mushrooms and place over medium-high heat. Scrape in the chickpea batter and "scramble" until cooked through, about 8 minutes.

4 To make the burritos, warm the tortillas in another nonstick skillet or in the oven. Cut the tomatoes and avocado into large dice.

5 Divide the tortillas among four plates, and top with equal amounts of the chickpea scramble, tomatoes, avocado, and mushrooms. Season each tortilla with kala namak and roll up into burritos.

TIP

These burritos also taste great filled with the Tofu Scramble on page 117.

"EGG SALAD" SANDWICH

BETTER THAN THE ORIGINAL

Preparation time 10 minutes • **Makes** 4 sandwiches

Chickpeas, soy cream, and spices are the base components for these sandwiches. Kala namak from India, also known as black salt, gives them an eggy flavor just like the original. Topped with sliced radishes, these make an ideal breakfast snack.

1½ cups (250 g) cooked chickpeas

2 tablespoons soy or another plant-based cream

1 teaspoon Dijon mustard

1½ teaspoons apple cider vinegar

¼ teaspoon ground turmeric

1 teaspoon kala namak (see Tip, page 63)

¼ teaspoon freshly ground black pepper

1 tablespoon oat milk

4 gluten-free whole grain sandwich rolls

4 radishes, thinly sliced

4 tablespoons minced fresh chives

1 Place half the chickpeas in a food processor. Add the soy cream, mustard, vinegar, turmeric, kala namak, and pepper and process until roughly chopped.

2 Mash the remaining chickpeas with the oat milk in a bowl. Add the chopped chickpeas and stir to combine into "egg salad."

3 Slice open the rolls and spread with the "egg salad." Garnish each with radish slices and chives.

GLUTEN FREE   SUGAR FREE

TIP

These sandwiches also taste great with sliced cucumbers, pickled beets, or tomatoes instead of radishes. Try them on our Whole Grain Rolls (page 171).

SESAME AMARANTH CRACKERS

FOR BITE-AND-GO MORNINGS

Preparation time 60 minutes • **Baking time** 25 minutes • **Makes** 35 to 40 crackers

Sometimes life goes even faster than usual, especially in the morning. So we always make sure to keep an airtight container of these crackers handy to spread with different toppings and enjoy on the go, or serve in a more leisurely way with coffee or tea.

⅔ cup (125 g) amaranth

¼ teaspoon salt

3 tablespoons sesame seeds

2 tablespoons chia seeds

1 Preheat the oven to 350°F (180°C). Line a baking sheet with parchment paper.

2 Place the amaranth in a pot with 1½ cups (350 ml) water and the salt and bring to a boil over medium heat. Cover the pot, lower the heat, and simmer for 25 minutes, or until the amaranth has absorbed all of the water. Stir in the sesame and chia seeds.

3 Place mounds of 1 to 2 teaspoonfuls of the batter on the prepared baking sheet. With moistened fingers, spread the batter out into thin rounds, 2 to 3 inches (5 to 7.5 cm) in diameter. Repeat with the remaining batter.

4 Bake for 15 minutes, then carefully flip all of the crackers and bake for another 10 minutes, or until they are crunchy and golden brown. Let cool on a wire rack and store in an airtight container.

TIP

These nutty crackers taste great no matter what you spread on them. But definitely try our Avocado Hummus on page 179.

HEARTY LENTIL MUFFINS
WITH CASHEW CREAM CHEESE

Preparation time 15 minutes • **Baking time** 20 minutes • **Makes** 12 muffins

The special flavor of these muffins comes from the combination of nutty brown lentils and fenugreek.

1¼ cups (150 g) spelt flour

¾ cup (100 g) buckwheat flour

1 tablespoon baking powder

2 tablespoons cornstarch

1 teaspoon salt

2 teaspoons fresh thyme leaves

2 teaspoons dried fenugreek leaves

½ teaspoon freshly ground black pepper

½ cup (100 ml) soy milk

⅓ cup (70 ml) olive oil, plus 1 tablespoon for the muffin pan

1 tablespoon agave syrup

2 ounces (50 g) smoked tofu (about a 2 × 2-inch/5 × 5 cm piece)

1 cup (200 g) cooked brown lentils

2 teaspoons chopped fresh flat-leaf parsley

2 tablespoons minced fresh chives

6 tablespoons Cashew Cream Cheese (page 179)

1 Preheat the oven to 320°F (160°C).

2 Whisk together the spelt flour, buckwheat flour, baking powder, cornstarch, salt, thyme, fenugreek, and pepper in a large bowl. In a separate bowl, whisk together the soy milk, ⅓ cup (70 ml) of olive oil, the agave syrup, and ¾ cup (200 ml) water. Whisk the wet ingredients into the dry ingredients and stir for 5 minutes, or until there are no lumps.

3 Dice the tofu into ¼-inch (5 mm) pieces. Fold the tofu, lentils, and parsley into the batter.

4 Brush a twelve-cup muffin pan with the remaining 1 tablespoon olive oil, then pour the batter evenly into each muffin cup. Bake for 20 minutes, or until a tester inserted in the middle of a muffin comes out clean.

5 Serve with the chives and cashew cream cheese.

TIP

To make these muffins crunchy, you can substitute a handful of chopped walnuts for the smoked tofu.

BREAKFAST BURGER
HANDHELD PROTEIN POWERHOUSE

Preparation time 25 minutes • **Cooking time** 20 minutes • **Makes** 4 burgers

A burger for breakfast sounds like a lot of work. But you can make the patties and even the tofu "egg" in advance, so all you need to do in the morning is briefly heat them in the pan. Delicious!

FOR THE PATTIES

2 tablespoons ground flaxseed

⅓ cup (75 g) millet

½ cup (100 g) cooked kidney beans

1 tablespoon chickpea flour

½ teaspoon ground cumin

½ teaspoon paprika

½ teaspoon dried oregano

¼ teaspoon salt

1 tablespoon olive oil

FOR THE TOFU "EGGS"

7 ounces (200 g) firm tofu

½ cup (120 ml) soy milk

1 tablespoon ground turmeric

¼ teaspoon freshly ground black pepper

1 teaspoon kala namak

1 tablespoon olive oil

FOR SERVING

4 gluten-free whole grain rolls or Whole Grain Rolls (page 171)

4 tablespoons prepared mustard

4 handfuls Swiss chard or spinach leaves, washed, dried, and cut into thin strips

1 To make the patties, mix the flaxseed with 2 tablespoons water and set aside to soak.

2 Cook the millet per the package instructions, or toast loose millet then simmer in ⅔ cup (160ml) water. Set aside to cool.

3 Place the millet, flaxseed, kidney beans, chickpea flour, cumin, paprika, oregano, and salt in a food processor and process until roughly chopped.

4 Pour the olive oil into a large nonstick skillet over medium-high heat. Form the patty mixture into four equal portions and cook them until golden brown, about 4 minutes on each side. Set aside, keeping warm.

5 To make the tofu "eggs," use a 3- to 4-inch (7.5 to 10 cm) cookie cutter or drinking glass to cut four round pieces (about 1 inch/2.5 cm thick) from the block of tofu. Set the rounds aside. Puree the remaining tofu with the soy milk, turmeric, pepper, and kala namak in a food processor or blender until smooth.

6 Pour the olive oil into the skillet used for the patties and warm over medium-high heat. Add the tofu rounds and cook until golden brown, about 4 minutes on each side. Set aside, keeping warm.

7 To serve, slice open the rolls and toast them, cut side down, in the hot skillet for about 2 minutes, until golden brown.

8 Spread each roll with 1 tablespoon mustard and layer on a patty, a tofu "egg," one quarter of the remaining tofu puree, and one quarter of the Swiss chard strips. Close the rolls and serve.

WAKE-UP POPSICLES

Preparation time 20 minutes • **Freezing time** 6 hours

light

You may think we're crazy for eating popsicles at breakfast, but we promise that these are just perfect for hot summer mornings. Grab one before leaving your house and stay cool—and full—all morning.

OATMEAL & RASPBERRY POPSICLES

Makes eight 2 × 4-inch (5 × 10 cm) popsicles

⅔ cup (50 g) rolled oats

¾ cup (200 ml) almond milk

1 cup (150 g) frozen raspberries

3 tablespoons agave syrup

2 tablespoons Cashew Butter (page 177)

⅔ cup (150 ml) coconut milk

1 Place the oats in a small pot over high heat and toast, stirring, for about 1 minute.

2 Stir in the almond milk and cook over low heat for 3 minutes.

3 Remove from the heat and let cool to room temperature.

4 Stir in the raspberries and agave syrup. In a separate bowl, gently stir together the cashew butter and coconut milk. Pour alternating dollops of oat-berry and cashew-coconut mixtures into eight popsicle molds.

5 Freeze for at least 6 hours.

BLUEBERRY POPSICLES

Makes eight 2 × 4-inch (5 × 10 cm) popsicles

1⅓ cups (200 g) fresh or frozen blueberries

3 tablespoons maple syrup

2 tablespoons Cashew Butter (page 177)

1¾ cups (400 g) plain soy yogurt

1 Place 1 cup (150 g) of the blueberries in a small pot. Add 2 tablespoons of the maple syrup. Cook over low heat for 15 minutes or until the blueberries have broken down.

2 Remove from the heat and let cool.

3 Combine the cashew butter, the remaining ⅓ cup (50 g) blueberries, the remaining 1 tablespoon maple syrup, and the yogurt in a small bowl.

4 Fill the eight popsicle molds three quarters with the yogurt mixture, then top with the blueberry compote.

5 Freeze for at least 6 hours.

STUFFED PARATHAS

WITH PEAS AND NIGELLA

balanced

Preparation time 30 minutes • **Makes** 2 parathas

Parathas are hearty stuffed flatbreads and an important part of every North Indian breakfast. They're a great way of using up leftover potatoes and taste just as good the next day.

FOR THE DOUGH

⅔ cup (75 g) spelt flour

⅔ cup (75 g) buckwheat flour

½ teaspoon salt

1 tablespoon olive oil

FOR THE FILLING

11 ounces (300 g) potatoes

Salt

½ medium yellow onion

¾ cup (100 g) fresh or frozen peas

1 teaspoon nigella seeds

¼ teaspoon ground turmeric

1 tablespoon vegetable oil

1. To make the dough, whisk together the spelt flour, buckwheat flour, and salt in a medium bowl. Add the olive oil and ½ cup (100 ml) lukewarm water, and knead until a smooth dough forms. Cover the bowl with plastic wrap and refrigerate until ready to use.

2. To make the filling, peel the potatoes and cut into 1-inch (2 cm) cubes. Place in a pot and cover with salted water. Bring to a boil and cook for 15 minutes, or until fork-tender.

3. Meanwhile, finely dice the onion.

4. Drain the potatoes and place them in a large bowl. Mash them roughly with a fork or potato masher. Mix in the onion, peas, nigella seeds, and turmeric. Add 1 teaspoon salt, or to taste.

5. Divide the dough into four equal portions. Roll and flatten each to a 6- to 8-inch (15 to 20 cm) round.

6. Place one quarter of the filling on each of the dough rounds, then fold the dough over to cover. Press around the edge to seal the parathas.

7. Pour the oil in a nonstick skillet over high heat. Sprinkle the parathas with a few drops of water, then place as many as you can fit at one time in the pan. Cover the pan with a lid and cook the parathas for 4 minutes, or until one side is golden brown and begins to fluff up. Uncover, flip the parathas, re-cover, and cook for another 4 minutes, or until completely fluffy and golden brown on both sides. Repeat with any remaining parathas. Serve, or let cool before wrapping.

TIP

Enjoy your parathas with a homemade Chai Latte with lots of milk (page 157).

CUCUMBER HUMMUS SANDWICHES

WITH CRUNCHY GREENS AND SPROUTS

Preparation time 15 minutes • **Makes** 4 sandwiches

Our cucumber hummus tastes particularly fresh and light. Since it's a breakfast food, we leave out the traditional garlic; this also helps makes these rolls easier to eat at the office or with friends.

½ English cucumber

1½ cups (250 g) cooked chickpeas

2 tablespoons tahini

½ teaspoon salt

Juice of ½ lemon

1 teaspoon minced fresh dill

¼ teaspoon freshly ground black pepper

4 gluten-free whole grain sandwich rolls

6 tablespoons fresh radish sprouts

6 cucumber slices

1 Wash the cucumber and chop into large chunks.

2 Place the cucumber, chickpeas, tahini, salt, lemon juice, dill, and pepper in a food processor or high-speed blender and process until smooth.

3 Slice open the rolls, spread with the hummus, and top with the radish sprouts and cucumber slices.

GLUTEN FREE   SUGAR FREE   SOY FREE

TIP

If you like sprouts and want to have them always handy, buy yourself a sprouting kit from the health food store. Growing them yourself is less expensive than buying them, and so much fun. Try them on Whole Grain Rolls (page 171).

ONE-BOWL WONDERS

QUINOA PORRIDGE
WITH CINNAMON AND ALMOND MILK

Preparation time 30 minutes • **Makes** 2 bowls

Quinoa contains a lot of plant protein and is high in iron, calcium, and magnesium. Its lightly nutty flavor and fluffy texture pair beautifully with fresh fruit, making it a great choice at breakfast that's filling but won't weigh you down.

½ cup (100 g) quinoa, rinsed and drained (see Tip)

¾ cup (200 ml) almond milk

1 teaspoon ground cinnamon

1 teaspoon maple syrup

2 tablespoons fresh or frozen raspberries

2 tablespoons fresh or frozen blueberries

2 tablespoons plain soy yogurt

GLUTEN FREE

1 Place the quinoa, almond milk, and ¾ cup (200 ml) water in a small pot and bring to a boil. Simmer over low heat for 25 minutes, uncovered, until the quinoa has absorbed all the liquid.

2 Fluff the quinoa with a fork. Gently stir in the cinnamon and maple syrup, then divide between two bowls.

3 Top with the berries and yogurt, and serve.

TIP

Always rinse quinoa a few times before cooking until the water runs clear. This removes the bitter taste from the natural saponin coating. Drain well before using.

GREEN SMOOTHIE BOWL

LICK-THE-BOWL-CLEAN GOOD

Preparation time 15 minutes • **Freezing time** 3 hours • **Resting time** 10 minutes • **Makes** 2 bowls

*A smoothie bowl is the easiest way to transform a smoothie into a full
and nutritious breakfast. Top with fresh fruit and lots of nourishing seeds for
a satisfying mouthful of green goodness.*

½ banana

½ peeled and pitted mango

1 kiwi (see Tips on page 37)

⅓ cup (50 g) fresh pineapple chunks

1 pitted Medjool date

1 handful baby spinach

FOR THE TOPPING

1 tablespoon hemp seeds

2 tablespoons fresh or frozen raspberries

1 tablespoon chia seeds

1 Peel the banana and cut into four equal pieces. Freeze for at least 3 hours.

2 Divide the mango piece in half and set aside one piece for the topping. Chop the remaining mango into chunks. Cut off the woody base of the kiwi and cut the kiwi in half. Place banana, mango, and kiwi in a food processor or high-speed blender with the pineapple, date, spinach, and ¾ cup (200 ml) water and process until smooth.

3 For the topping, cut the remaining mango piece into thin slices. Lightly crush the hemp seeds with a mortar and pestle.

4 Divide the smoothie between two bowls and top with the mango, hemp seeds, raspberries, and chia seeds. Allow the chia to swell for 10 minutes before serving.

TIP

Do you need an even more filling breakfast? Top the
smoothie bowl with a few tablespoons of rolled oats.

BIRCHER MUESLI

A VEGAN TAKE ON THE SWISS CLASSIC

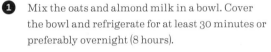

Preparation time 10 minutes • **Soaking time** 30 minutes to 8 hours • **Makes** 2 bowls

Rolled oats soaked in almond milk nearly melt in your mouth.
Grated apple and fresh berries add a fresh and fruity note.

½ cup (40 g) quick-cooking oats

¾ cup (200 ml) almond milk

2 small tart apples

¼ teaspoon ground cinnamon, plus 2 pinches

1 cup (250 g) plain soy yogurt

1 tablespoon fresh raspberries

1 tablespoon fresh blueberries

1 tablespoon maple syrup

8 raw almonds, roughly chopped

GLUTEN FREE

1 Mix the oats and almond milk in a bowl. Cover the bowl and refrigerate for at least 30 minutes or preferably overnight (8 hours).

2 When you're ready to eat, grate the apples and stir into the oats. Mix in ¼ teaspoon cinnamon.

3 Divide the muesli between two bowls and top with the yogurt, raspberries, blueberries, maple syrup, chopped almonds, and a pinch cinnamon each.

TIP

Bircher muesli was invented by a true health food pioneer in Switzerland and could be considered the original overnight oats. Today, you can garnish your vegan muesli with any combination of fruits and nuts you desire.

AMARANTH PORRIDGE
WITH CINNAMON-APPLE COMPOTE

Preparation time 25 minutes • **Makes** 2 bowls

*Fresh ginger in this amaranth porridge will warm you from the inside out.
It's a great breakfast for cold, wet autumn and winter days.*

⅔ cup (125 g) amaranth

1 apple, cored and finely diced

1 tablespoon coconut sugar

¾ teaspoon ground cinnamon

¼ teaspoon grated fresh ginger

2 dried figs, sliced

¼ cup (50 ml) almond milk

(GLUTEN FREE) (SUGAR FREE) (SOY FREE)

1. Place the amaranth and 1¼ cups (300 ml) water in a small pot and bring to a boil over medium-high heat. Lower the heat, put the lid on the pot slightly askew, and simmer for 20 minutes.

2. Meanwhile, place the apple, coconut sugar, ¼ cup (50 ml) water, cinnamon, and ginger in a separate pot. Bring to a boil over medium-high heat, then lower the heat, cover the pot, and simmer for 20 minutes.

3. Divide the amaranth between two bowls. Top with the apple compote, sliced figs, and almond milk.

TIP

You can make the apple compote a day in advance and warm it up just before serving. You can also store it in the freezer.

BERRY SMOOTHIE BOWL

EAT THE RAINBOW

Preparation time 10 minutes • **Freezing time** 3 hours • **Makes** 2 bowls

In summer, the berry selection at farmers' markets and at local pick-it-yourself farms explodes. And depending on where you live, you might even have raspberries or blackberries growing wild in your backyard, in fields, and on the edges of forests. No matter where you find your fresh berries, a smoothie bowl made with fresh berries is the most refreshing breakfast on hot summer days.

1 banana

¾ cup (100 g) fresh or frozen raspberries

⅔ cup (100 g) fresh or frozen blackberries

1 handful baby spinach

1 tablespoon unsweetened dried cranberries

1 teaspoon hemp seeds

1 teaspoon rolled oats

1 Peel the banana and cut into four equal pieces. Freeze for at least 3 hours.

2 Place the banana, raspberries, blackberries, spinach, cranberries, and ¾ cup (200 ml) water in a food processor or high-speed blender and process until smooth.

3 Roughly crush the hemp seeds with a mortar and pestle. Toast the oats in a small hot dry skillet for about 1 minute, stirring constantly, until golden brown.

4 Divide the smoothie between two bowls and top with the hemp seeds and oats.

TIP

Frozen berries still contain a lot of vitamins. So even if they're not in season, you can always rest easy with frozen berries in the freezer.

MISO OATMEAL

AN UMAMI BURST TO YOUR BREAKFAST ROUTINE

Cooking time 15 minutes • **Makes** 2

*If you like the idea of a savory take on your morning oats,
try this miso oatmeal with toasty sesame oil and peas.*

1 teaspoon toasted sesame oil

1 teaspoon olive oil

1¼ cups (100 g) rolled oats

⅓ cup (50 g) frozen peas

1 tablespoon white miso

1 tablespoon soy sauce

1 scallion, green part only, sliced into thin rings

1 Place the sesame oil, olive oil, and oats in a small heavy pot over medium-high heat. Toast the oats for about 2 minutes, stirring continuously, until golden brown.

2 Stir in the peas, lower the heat, and let cook for another minute.

3 Stir in 1½ cups (350 ml) water, put the lid on the pot askew, and simmer for about 8 minutes, stirring often, until the oats are soft and thickened.

4 Remove the pot from the heat and stir in the miso and soy sauce. Divide between two bowls and garnish with the scallion. Serve immediately.

TIP

If you're afraid of scallion breath in the morning,
replace it with 2 tablespoons toasted sesame seeds
for a scent-free crunch.

COCONUT CHIA PUDDING
WITH BANANAS AND BERRIES

Preparation time 10 minutes • **Resting time** 8 hours • **Makes** 2 bowls

*Creamy coconut milk and nutritious chia seeds make an indulgent pudding
in no time, and it tastes particularly good when topped with fresh fruit.
A perfect breakfast for people in a hurry.*

3 tablespoons chia seeds

¾ cup (200 ml) coconut milk (see Tip)

1 banana, sliced

1 handful fresh or frozen raspberries

1 handful fresh or frozen blackberries

1 Mix the chia seeds and coconut milk together in a medium bowl. Cover and refrigerate overnight (8 hours).

2 The next morning, divide the pudding between two bowls. Garnish with the banana, raspberries, and blackberries and serve immediately.

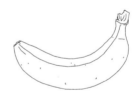

TIP

Instead of coconut milk, you can use whatever
nut or soy milk you like. Since coconut milk is thicker
than other plant-based milks, use a little less nut or
soy milk than called for to make sure your pudding
isn't too thin.

CHOCOLATE-FOR-BREAKFAST PORRIDGE

WITH BANANAS AND NUTS

Cooking time 20 minutes • **Makes** 2 servings

*Sweet bananas are a great companion to dark and hearty cacao and make
for pure energy in a glass or a bowl, however you prefer.*

1¼ cups (100 g) rolled oats

1¼ cups (300 ml) oat milk

2 tablespoons raw cacao powder

2 tablespoons maple syrup

1 tablespoon raw almonds

1 tablespoon raw hazelnuts

1 banana

1 tablespoon unsweetened shredded coconut

1 Place the oats, milk and ¾ cup (200 ml) water in a small pot over medium-high heat and bring to a boil. Lower the heat and put the lid on the pot askew. Simmer for about 10 minutes, stirring occasionally, until the oats are soft and thickened.

2 Remove from the heat and stir in the cacao and maple syrup.

3 Roughly chop the almonds and hazelnuts. Peel and slice the banana.

4 Divide the porridge between two bowls or tall glasses and garnish with the nuts, banana, and coconut.

TIP

This porridge also makes a great and easy dessert,
or dessert for breakfast!

BANANA PUDDING
WITH SUPER MUESLI

 light

Preparation time 10 minutes • **Makes** 2 servings

Our deliciously creamy banana pudding is pretty great on its own, but mixing it with your favorite granola, muesli, or fruits and nuts takes it to the next level.

2 ripe bananas, cut into chunks

⅔ cup (150 ml) oat milk

3 tablespoons raw cashews

3 tablespoons chia seeds

¾ teaspoon ground cardamom

2 tablespoons Bircher Muesli (page 85)

GLUTEN FREE   SOY FREE

Place the bananas, oat milk, cashews, chia seeds, and cardamom in a food processor or high-speed blender. Process until smooth. Divide the pudding between two bowls and top with the muesli.

TIP

In the summer, make this even more refreshing by using frozen bananas. Or chill the finished pudding for 30 minutes before serving; just mix in ½ teaspoon lemon juice per bowl beforehand so the pudding doesn't turn brown.

BUCKWHEAT PORRIDGE
WITH FRESH BERRIES

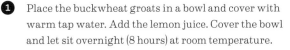

Preparation time 15 minutes • **Soaking time** 8 hours • **Makes** 2 bowls

*Buckwheat is a great source of protein, and helps get your brain going in the morning.
Our raw porridge needs no cooking and comes together quickly.*

⅔ cup (100 g) buckwheat groats

1 teaspoon fresh lemon juice

3 tablespoons almond milk

½ teaspoon ground cinnamon

1 tablespoon maple syrup

1 tablespoon plus 1 teaspoon unsweetened shredded coconut

2 tablespoons pomegranate seeds (see Tip, page 29)

1 tablespoon fresh or frozen blueberries (see Tip)

1 teaspoon chia seeds

1 Place the buckwheat groats in a bowl and cover with warm tap water. Add the lemon juice. Cover the bowl and let sit overnight (8 hours) at room temperature.

2 The next morning, drain the buckwheat, which will have become somewhat viscous, rinse it, and drain again. Place the buckwheat, almond milk, cinnamon, maple syrup, and 1 tablespoon of the coconut in a food processor or high-speed blender and process until smooth.

3 Divide among four bowls and top with the pomegranate seeds, blueberries, the remaining coconut, and the chia seeds. Allow the chia seeds to swell for 10 minutes before serving.

TIP

You can use whatever berry you like as a garnish in this recipe. If you prefer, you can add the berries directly to the blender before processing.

MILLET QUINOA PORRIDGE
THE GLUTEN-FREE FITNESS BOOSTER

light

Preparation time 20 minutes • **Makes** 2 bowls

Finely ground and cooked together, millet and quinoa are filling power grains that make a wonderfully creamy breakfast cereal.

¼ cup (50 g) millet

⅓ cup (50 g) quinoa, rinsed and drained (See Tip, page 81)

Pinch of salt

¼ cup (50 ml) almond milk

½ teaspoon ground cinnamon

1 pear, cored and sliced

1 handful fresh or frozen raspberries

GLUTEN FREE • SUGAR FREE • SOY FREE

1 Place the millet and quinoa in a small food processor, clean coffee grinder, or high-speed blender and process until roughly ground.

2 Place 2 cups (500 ml) water in a small pot and bring to a boil. Stir in the ground millet and quinoa and the salt. Lower the heat, cover the pot with a lid, and let simmer. After about 8 minutes, stir in the almond milk. Cook for 2 minutes more.

3 Stir in the cinnamon and remove the pot from the heat. Let sit, covered, for 2 minutes.

4 Divide the porridge into two bowls and top with the pear and raspberries.

TIP

You can use different gluten-free grains here, like amaranth or brown rice (but adjust the cooking time per package instructions). Experiment and find your favorite combination.

'NANA NICE CREAM

WITH OVERNIGHT OATS AND CHIA CREAM

balanced

Preparation time 15 minutes • **Soaking time** 8 hours • **Freezing time** 20 minutes • **Makes** 2 servings

*Bananas are the base for this unbelievably creamy vegan ice cream.
Combined with classic overnight oats and a coconutty chia cream, they make a pretty
fantastic, completely unboring summer breakfast.*

FOR THE OVERNIGHT OATS

¼ cup (20 g) rolled oats

⅓ cup (75 ml) almond milk

1 teaspoon maple syrup (optional)

FOR THE NICE CREAM

2 bananas

1 tablespoon Cashew Butter (page 177)

½ teaspoon ground cinnamon

¼ teaspoon ground cardamom

Pinch of salt

FOR THE CHIA CREAM

2 tablespoons chia seeds

½ cup (100 ml) coconut milk

1 kiwi

1 To make the overnight oats, mix together the oats, almond milk, and maple syrup (if using) in a medium bowl. Cover the bowl and let soak overnight (8 hours) in the fridge.

2 While the oats are soaking, peel the banana, cut into four equal pieces, and freeze for at least 3 hours.

3 To make the nice cream, the next morning, place the bananas, cashew butter, cinnamon, cardamom, and salt in a food processor or high-speed blender and process until smooth. Pour into a freezer container and freeze for about 20 minutes to firm up.

4 To make the chia cream, stir together the chia seeds and coconut milk. Set aside for at least 15 minutes for the seeds to swell.

5 Slice the kiwi.

6 Pour a layer of nice cream into the bottom of two tumblers, then cover with a layer of chia cream. Layer on kiwi slices and some overnight oats, then top with another layer of nice cream. Serve immediately.

TIP

If you don't know what to do with overripe bananas, just peel and slice them, then freeze them. You can use them directly from the freezer for smoothies or in this nice cream recipe.

BLACK CHAI RICE
WITH FRUIT AND COCONUT TOPPING

Preparation time 40 minutes • **Makes** 2 bowls

Legend has it that after eating black rice, one is blessed with good ideas. It's one of the reasons why in ancient times only the Emperor of China was allowed to eat it and it became known as forbidden rice. Luckily, these days everyone can enjoy it. We're crossing our fingers that this breakfast will conjure many great ideas for you, too!

⅔ cup (125 g) black rice

½ cup (100 ml) coconut milk

1 chai tea bag

½ mango, peeled and sliced

1 kiwi, cut into wedges

1 tablespoon goji berries

1 tablespoon coconut flakes

1 teaspoon chia seeds

1 tablespoon agave syrup

1 Rinse the rice under running water until the water runs clear. Place the rice, coconut milk, ½ cup (100 ml) water, and the tea bag in a small pot and bring to a boil. Lower the heat, cover the pot, and simmer for 35 minutes, stirring occasionally. Remove and discard the tea bag.

2 Divide the rice between two bowls and top with the mango, kiwi, goji berries, coconut flakes, and chia seeds. Drizzle with additional coconut milk and the agave syrup. Serve immediately.

GLUTEN FREE **SUGAR FREE** **SOY FREE**

TIP

You can make the rice the evening before you plan to serve it and assemble the bowls the next day. To do so, let the rice cool completely before storing it in the fridge. You can serve the finished bowls warm (simply reheat on the stove or in the microwave) or cold.

UNBORING FRUIT SALAD BOWL
WITH COCONUT PUDDING

Preparation time 15 minutes • **Resting time** 1 hour • **Makes** 2 bowls

Fruit salad is a quick and easy thing to prepare for breakfast—but fruit on its own can be a little too light. Combine it with coconut pudding, though, and you get a filling, crunchy, and colorful breakfast that's as photogenic as it is delicious.

¼ cup (50 g) chia seeds

1¼ cups (300 ml) coconut milk

3 tablespoons coconut chips

1 banana

½ grapefruit

2 kiwis (see Tip, page 37)

4 fresh strawberries

⅓ cup (50 g) fresh pineapple chunks

3 tablespoons fresh blueberries

3 tablespoons fresh raspberries

1. Mix the chia seeds and coconut milk together in a bowl and let rest for at least 1 hour in the fridge.

2. Meanwhile, toast the coconut chips in a hot dry skillet for about 3 minutes, stirring, until golden brown. Let cool, then mix into the pudding.

3. Peel and slice the banana. Peel the grapefruit and cut into segments. Cut off woody base and dice the kiwis and the strawberries.

4. Divide the pudding between two bowls. Arrange the bananas, grapefruit, kiwis, strawberries, pineapple, blueberries, and raspberries on top and serve.

HOT OFF THE STOVE

POPPY SEED PANCAKES
DELICIOUSLY BITE-SIZED AND SOFT

Preparation time 15 minutes • **Cooking time** 20 minutes • **Makes** 12 pancakes

Pancakes are a classic at the American breakfast table. Ours are gluten-free and crammed with crunchy poppy seeds and other nutritious ingredients, which makes them much lighter than the typical flapjack.

1¾ cup (150 g) rolled oats

¾ cup plus 1 tablespoon (130 g) rice flour

1½ teaspoons baking powder

½ teaspoon baking soda

2 tablespoons poppy seeds

2 teaspoons maple syrup

6 tablespoons unsweetened applesauce

⅔ cup (150 ml) almond milk

¾ cup (175 ml) sparkling water

Pinch of salt

1 tablespoon coconut oil, melted

1 Preheat the oven to 200°F (95°C).

2 Place the oats in a food processor, clean coffee grinder, or high-speed blender and process until finely ground. Pour into a large bowl. Add the rice flour, baking powder, baking soda, poppy seeds, maple syrup, applesauce, almond milk, sparkling water, and salt. Whisk until the batter is smooth.

3 Drizzle the coconut oil in a large skillet over medium heat. Use a ¼-cup (60 ml) measure to spoon pancake batter into rounds in the pan. Cook on both sides until golden brown, about 3 minutes per side. Keep the prepared pancakes warm in the oven while you cook the remaining pancakes.

TIP

These pancakes turn downright decadent when served with a dollop of our Berry Chia Jam (page 177) and a drizzle of maple syrup.

TOFU OMELET
WITH ROASTED CHERRY TOMATOES

balanced

Cooking time 45 minutes • **Makes** 2 omelets

You don't have to give up savory, fluffy omelets if you're a vegan. Silken tofu and our favorite secret weapon—kala namak—are transformed into a light and airy twist on the classic that we like to stuff with roasted cherry tomatoes. They'll knock your socks off.

FOR THE ROASTED TOMATOES

9 ounces (250 g) cherry tomatoes

2 teaspoons olive oil

1 teaspoon coarse salt

½ teaspoon fresh thyme leaves

FOR THE OMELET

7 ounces (200 g) silken tofu, drained

½ cup (50 g) chickpea flour

1½ tablespoons rolled oats

1 tablespoon tapioca starch

½ teaspoon ground turmeric

¼ teaspoon salt

1 tablespoon olive oil

¼ teaspoon kala namak

2 tablespoons chopped fresh flat-leaf parsley

1 Preheat the oven to 400°F (200°C).

2 To make the roasted tomatoes, place the cherry tomatoes in a baking dish in one layer. Drizzle with the olive oil and sprinkle with the coarse salt and thyme. Mix well to coat. Roast for 25 minutes. Remove from the oven and set aside.

3 Meanwhile, to make the omelet, place the tofu, chickpea flour, oats, tapioca starch, turmeric, and salt in a food processor and process until fully blended.

4 Put 1½ teaspoons of the olive oil in a nonstick skillet over medium-high heat. Pour half of the tofu mixture into the pan and cook for 4 minutes or until slightly browned. Flip and cook for another 4 minutes. Remove from the pan and set aside, keeping warm. Repeat with the remaining oil and tofu mixture for the second omelet.

5 Place the omelets on two plates. Arrange half of the roasted tomatoes on each, season with kala namak, and fold the omelet in half before serving. Garnish with the parsley.

TIP

During roasting, tomatoes develop a sweet, caramelized flavor and melt-in-your-mouth texture. Don't skip the roasting unless you are running out the door—but in that case you may find one of our Breakfast To Go recipes (pages 57–77) easier to manage.

BUCKWHEAT CRÊPES
A CINNAMON-FLAVORED TREAT

Cooking time 40 minutes • **Makes** 6 crêpes

The best crêpes are freshly made, golden brown, and lacy-thin. We put a hint of cinnamon in our delicate Buckwheat Crêpes, which taste great at any time of day, not just breakfast.

¾ cup (100 g) buckwheat flour

3 tablespoons tapioca starch

1 teaspoon ground cinnamon

½ teaspoon baking powder

Pinch of salt

½ cup (100 ml) almond milk

1½ teaspoons coconut oil

½ cup (100 g) plain soy yogurt

⅔ cup (100 g) fresh blueberries

2 tablespoons maple syrup

GLUTEN FREE

1 Preheat the oven to 200°F (95°C).

2 Whisk together the buckwheat flour, tapioca starch, cinnamon, baking powder and salt in a medium bowl. In a separate bowl, combine the almond milk with ¾ cup (200 ml) water. Pour the wet ingredients into the dry ingredients and whisk until smooth.

3 Melt ¼ teaspoon of the coconut oil in a nonstick skillet over medium-high heat. Use a ¼ -cup (60 ml) measure to pour crêpe batter into the pan. Tilt the pan so the batter spreads in a thin, even layer over the whole surface. Cook the crêpe until golden brown on both sides, 2 to 3 minutes for each side. Remove the crêpe from the pan and place on a baking sheet in the oven to keep warm. Repeat with the remaining coconut oil and batter.

4 Divide the crêpes between two plates. Serve topped with yogurt, blueberries, and maple syrup.

TIP

If you leave out the cinnamon, you can serve these crêpes with savory toppings, too. We are partial to spinach sautéed quickly in a drizzle of olive oil.

TOFU SCRAMBLE

WITH TURMERIC AND KALA NAMAK

balanced

Cooking time 30 minutes • **Makes** 2 servings

Scrambled eggs remind us of our childhood. For lots of amateur cooks, they're the first dish they learned to cook. Our Tofu Scramble is just as easy as, and even more satisfying than, the classic you, too, may have grown up with.

1 medium yellow onion

3 tablespoons olive oil

One 14-ounce (400 g) package medium-firm tofu, drained and pressed

½ teaspoon salt

1 teaspoon ground turmeric

¼ cup (55 g) plain soy yogurt

¼ teaspoon freshly ground black pepper

½ teaspoon kala namak

3 tablespoons minced chives

1 Peel and dice the onion.

2 Pour the olive oil in a nonstick skillet over medium-high heat. Sauté the onion for about 4 minutes, stirring occasionally, until translucent.

3 Crumble the tofu into a bowl with your fingers. Add to the onion along with the salt and turmeric. Sauté for about 7 minutes.

4 Remove from the heat. Stir in the yogurt, pepper, and kala namak.

5 Divide between two plates. Garnish with the chives and serve immediately.

(GLUTEN FREE)　(SUGAR FREE)

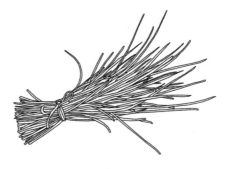

TIP

For a smokier flavor, replace the plain tofu with smoked tofu and sauté until it's crispy. This scramble is also great with our Rye Sourdough Bread (page 169).

POWER WAFFLES
WITH BERRY COMPOTE

balanced

Cooking time 30 minutes • **Makes** 8 waffles

Our Power Waffles are full of nourishing ingredients and will give you plenty of energy for your day. For busy mornings, we recommend making the batter the night before.

FOR THE COMPOTE

1½ cups (200 g) fresh or frozen mixed berries

1 tablespoon agave syrup

1 tablespoon chia seeds

FOR THE WAFFLES

¼ cup (50 g) millet

⅓ cup (50 g) flaxseed

¼ cup (30 g) raw almonds

1¼ cups (100 g) rolled oats

3 tablespoons unsweetened applesauce

1 cup (225 ml) almond milk

About 3 tablespoons sesame seeds

(GLUTEN FREE) (SUGAR FREE) (SOY FREE)

1 To make the compote, place the berries and agave syrup in a small pot over medium heat and bring to a boil. Lower the heat and simmer for 10 minutes.

2 Remove from the heat and let cool for 10 minutes; stir in the chia seeds. Set aside.

3 Preheat the oven to 200°F (95°C).

4 To make the waffles, place the millet and flaxseed in a mini food processor, clean coffee grinder, or high-speed blender and grind until fine.

5 Add 1 cup (225 ml) water, the almonds, oats, applesauce, and almond milk and process until smooth.

6 Heat a waffle iron to 400°F (200°C). Sprinkle a few sesame seeds in the iron. Evenly spread 3 to 4 tablespoons of the waffle batter in the iron, then sprinkle more sesame seeds on top. Cook the waffles until golden brown, about 5 minutes. Keep warm in the oven while you repeat with the remaining seeds and batter.

7 Serve with the berry compote.

TIP

Compote made with fresh fruit is a much healthier and tastier alternative to the traditional maple syrup to sweeten these. In place of the berry compote, you could also serve these with Apple Butter (page 177) or a dollop of soy yogurt.

SPELT-RICE CRÊPES

WITH GREENS AND WILD HERBS

balanced

Preparation time 5 minutes • **Cooking time** 20 minutes • **Makes** 4 crêpes

*These thin crêpes are made with rice and spelt flour and a touch of coconut,
then filled with delicate wild herbs and homemade cashew parmesan cheese.
We promise you've never had anything like it.*

⅔ cup (100 g) rice flour

¾ cup plus 1 tablespoon (100 g) spelt flour

¾ cup (190 ml) coconut milk

½ teaspoon ground turmeric

½ teaspoon salt

Mixed wild herbs, such as dandelions, wild garlic, spinach, or sorrel, washed and roughly chopped (about 4 cups/120 g; see Tip)

2 tablespoons olive oil

FOR THE CASHEW "PARMESAN"

2½ tablespoons raw cashews

2½ tablespoons nutritional yeast flakes

1 teaspoon salt

(SUGAR FREE) (SOY FREE)

1 Whisk together the rice flour, spelt flour, coconut milk, ¾ cup (190 ml) water, turmeric, and salt together in a bowl to make a thin batter.

2 To make the cashew "parmesan," finely grind the cashews, nutritional yeast, and salt with a mortar and pestle or in a food processor.

3 If you will be serving the crêpes all at the same time, preheat the oven to 200°F (95°C). Line a baking sheet with parchment paper.

4 Pour 1½ teaspoons of the olive oil in an 11-inch (28 cm) nonstick skillet over medium-high heat. Pour one quarter of the batter into the pan and spread it out with the back of a ladle or spatula to cover the surface. Cook for 2 minutes over high heat.

5 Top with a generous handful of the herbs. Spread 1 tablespoon of the cashew "parmesan" on the crêpe. Cover the pan with a lid and cook for another 3 minutes.

6 Take the lid off, fold the crêpe in half, and garnish with more wild herbs. Repeat with remaining oil, batter, herbs, and cashew "parmesan." Place the crêpes on the baking sheet in the oven to keep warm while you're making the rest. Serve hot.

TIP

It's not always easy to find fresh and tasty wild herbs. So you can also try making these with fresh baby spinach, radish greens, or Swiss chard, or use herbs that you froze during the summer.

THE SWEETER SIDE OF MORNINGS

CARROT CUPCAKES

WITH CASHEW–POPPY SEED FROSTING

Preparation time 35 minutes • **Soaking time** 8 hours • **Baking time** 20 minutes • **Chilling time** 15 minutes • **Makes** 12 cupcakes

We think everyone should indulge every once in a while, even at breakfast, when the craving calls. Our inspiration for this particular recipe came from a quick trip to Prague, where we had them in a small vegan restaurant.

FOR THE FROSTING

1 cup (150 g) raw cashews

½ cup (100 ml) coconut oil

¼ cup (50 g) plain soy yogurt

Grated zest of ½ lemon

2 tablespoons fresh lemon juice

1 tablespoon maple syrup

2 tablespoons poppy seeds

FOR THE CUPCAKES

1 tablespoon vegetable oil

2 small carrots (3½ ounces/100 g)

1⅔ cups (200 g) spelt flour

½ cup (100 g) raw sugar

2 teaspoons ground cinnamon

1 teaspoon baking powder

1 teaspoon baking soda

½ cup (100 ml) canola oil

⅔ cup (150 g) unsweetened applesauce

3 tablespoons almond butter

½ teaspoon grated fresh ginger

1. To start making the frosting, soak the cashews in water overnight (8 hours) in a covered container in the fridge.

2. In the morning, drain the cashews, rinse, and drain again. Set aside until you're ready to make the frosting.

3. To make the cupcakes, preheat the oven to 350°F (180°C). Grease a twelve-cup muffin pan with the vegetable oil.

4. Finely grate the carrots by hand or in a food processor.

5. Whisk together the spelt flour, sugar, cinnamon, baking powder, and baking soda in a medium bowl. In a separate bowl, whisk together the canola oil, applesauce, almond butter, and ginger. Pour the wet ingredients into the dry ingredients and whisk until smooth. Stir in the grated carrots.

6. Pour the batter into the prepared pan (fill the cups ⅔ full). Bake for 20 minutes. A cake tester inserted into the center of a cupcake should come out clean. Remove from the oven and let cool completely on a wire rack.

7. To finish making the frosting, while the cupcakes are cooling, melt the coconut oil in a small pot over low heat. Place the reserved cashews, the coconut oil, yogurt, lemon zest and juice, and maple syrup in a food processor or high-speed blender and process until smooth. Stir in the poppy seeds.

8. Scrape the frosting into a piping bag or ziplock bag with a hole snipped in a corner. Chill in the freezer for at least 15 minutes.

9. Pipe the chilled frosting on top of the cooled cupcakes.

BLUEBERRY BLONDIES
FRUITY AND GLUTEN-FREE

Preparation time 30 minutes • **Baking time** 45 minutes • **Makes** 12 blondies

Blondies are a lighter version of brownies, and with the fresh blueberries they're perfect for breakfast or brunch.

2 tablespoons coconut oil

¾ cup plus 1 tablespoon (100 g) coconut flour

⅔ cup (80 g) tapioca starch

⅓ cup (80 g) coconut sugar

1 teaspoon grated lemon zest

1 tablespoon baking powder

¼ teaspoon salt

2 tablespoons fresh lemon juice

¾ cup (180 g) unsweetened applesauce

⅔ cup (150 ml) almond milk

⅔ cup (100 g) fresh or frozen blueberries

1 Preheat the oven to 350°F (180°C). Grease a 9 × 13-inch (23 × 33 cm) baking dish with 1 tablespoon of the coconut oil.

2 Whisk together the coconut flour, tapioca starch, coconut sugar, lemon zest, baking powder, and salt in a medium bowl. In a separate bowl, whisk together the lemon juice, applesauce, almond milk, and the remaining 1 tablespoon coconut oil (melted). Pour the wet ingredients into the dry ingredients and whisk until smooth. Gently fold in the blueberries. Scrape the batter into the baking dish and smooth the top.

3 Bake for 45 minutes, or until the blondies are firm to the touch and a cake tester inserted into the center comes out clean.

4 Let cool completely in the pan. Cut into twelve pieces.

TIP

In the summer, these also taste great made with pitted fresh cherries.

RAW CHEESECAKE TARTLETS
WITH FRESH STRAWBERRIES

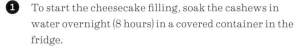

Preparation time 20 minutes • **Soaking time** 8 hours • **Chilling time** 30 minutes • **Makes** three 3-inch (7.5 cm) tartlets

Don't these little tarts look fancy? If you want to impress your friends and family, these are the way to go. Deliciously decadent!

FOR THE CHEESECAKE FILLING

1½ cups (200 g) raw cashews

1½ tablespoons coconut oil

2 tablespoons agave syrup

3 tablespoons almond milk

⅔ cup (100 g) fresh or frozen strawberries

Juice of ½ lemon

FOR THE BASE

5 pitted Medjool dates

⅔ cup (85 g) raw almonds

1 tablespoon coconut oil

1½ teaspoons raw cacao powder

1½ teaspoons maple syrup

⅔ cup (100 g) fresh or frozen strawberries

1 To start the cheesecake filling, soak the cashews in water overnight (8 hours) in a covered container in the fridge.

2 In the morning, drain the cashews, rinse, and drain again. Set aside.

3 To make the base, place the dates, almonds, coconut oil, cacao, and maple syrup in a food processor and process until finely ground and well combined. Divide the mixture among three 3-inch (7.5 cm) tartlet pans or dessert rings on a baking sheet and press down firmly.

4 To finish the cheesecake filling, place the cashews, coconut oil, agave syrup, almond milk, strawberries, and lemon juice in a food processor or high-speed blender and process until smooth.

5 Scrape the filling into the three tartlet pans on top of the base, and smooth the top. Chill in the fridge for at least 30 minutes.

6 Carefully press the tartlets out of the pans or remove the rings. Arrange the whole strawberries on top of the tartlets.

TIP

In the summer, you can make these tartlets with fresh raspberries. The tartlets are especially refreshing if you chill them for 20 minutes in the freezer.

GLAZED BAKED DONUTS

A HOLE IN ONE!

Preparation time 30 minutes • **Baking time** 10 minutes • **Makes** 6 donuts

*Usually donuts are deep-fried, but here we give you a healthier, lighter way of making them.
Finally, you can enjoy donuts for breakfast—guilt-free!*

FOR THE DONUTS

2 tablespoons coconut oil

1 tablespoon ground flaxseed

¾ cup plus 1 tablespoon (100 g) spelt flour

½ teaspoon baking powder

¼ teaspoon salt

7 tablespoons agave syrup

½ cup (100 ml) almond milk

FOR THE CHOCOLATE GLAZE

1½ teaspoons coconut oil

1½ teaspoons raw cacao powder

1½ teaspoons maple syrup

Pinch of salt

FOR DECORATION

1 tablespoon Berry Chia Jam (page 177)

1 tablespoon roughly chopped raw hazelnuts

1 tablespoon roughly chopped pistachios

① To make the donuts, preheat the oven to 350°F (180°C). Grease a donut baking pan with 1 tablespoon of the coconut oil.

② Mix the flaxseed with 1 tablespoon water in a medium bowl and set aside for 10 minutes.

③ Whisk together the spelt flour, baking powder, and salt in another medium bowl. Add the agave syrup, almond milk, and the remaining 1 tablespoon coconut oil to the flaxseed and whisk together. Whisk the wet ingredients into the dry ingredients until smooth and no lumps remain.

④ Pour the batter into the prepared pan. Bake for 10 minutes, or until a cake tester inserted into one of the donuts comes out clean. Let cool for 5 minutes in the pan, then gently tap to remove them and transfer to a wire rack to cool completely.

⑤ To make, the chocolate glaze, melt the coconut oil in a small skillet. Whisk in the cacao, maple syrup, and salt.

⑥ To decorate, drizzle the glaze on two of the donuts and top with the hazelnuts.

⑦ Spread two more donuts with jam and sprinkle with the pistachios. Leave the remaining donuts plain.

TIP

You can also leave all the donuts plain and use the glaze and jam as a dip.

RAW CARROT CAKE
WITH LEMONY CASHEW FROSTING

comfort food

Preparation time 20 minutes • **Soaking time** 8 hours • **Chilling time** 30 minutes • **Makes** one 6-inch (15 cm) cake

Raw cakes are perfect for breakfast: You don't have to worry about burning them in the oven, and they stay fresh for several days in the fridge. This raw carrot cake also happens to be very healthy, with no added sugar, so you can enjoy it at breakfast guilt-free.

FOR THE CASHEW FROSTING

¾ cup (100 g) raw cashews

½ vanilla bean

2 tablespoons solid coconut oil

2 tablespoons maple syrup

1 tablespoon fresh lemon juice

FOR THE CAKE

1 tablespoon solid coconut oil

2 medium carrots (4½ ounces/125 g)

Generous ½ cup (80 g) raw almonds

½ cup (80 g) pitted Medjool dates

⅓ cup (25 g) unsweetened shredded coconut

2½ teaspoons ground cinnamon

¼ teaspoon grated fresh ginger

GLUTEN FREE   SOY FREE

① To start the frosting, soak the cashews in water overnight (8 hours) in a covered container in the fridge.

② In the morning, drain the cashews, rinse, and drain again.

③ To make the cake, grease a 6-inch (15 cm) round cake pan with the coconut oil.

④ Grate the carrots by hand or in a food processor. Scrape them into a large bowl. (No need to wash the food processor.)

⑤ Place the almonds and dates in the food processor and process until finely chopped. Add to the carrots along with the coconut, ½ teaspoon of the cinnamon, and the ginger. Mix well. Using your hands, press the mixture into the prepared pan in an even layer.

⑥ To finish the frosting, split the vanilla bean open lengthwise and scrape the seeds out with a knife. Set aside the pod.

⑦ Place the cashews, vanilla seeds, coconut oil, maple syrup, lemon juice, and 2 tablespoons water in a food processor or high-speed blender, and process until smooth. Spread evenly over the cake.

⑧ Chill the cake in the fridge for at least 30 minutes before serving. Dust with the remaining 2 teaspoons cinnamon.

TIP

You can also make the cake in a loaf pan, making neat slices you can pack in your lunch box. The cake works as great as dessert as for breakfast!

LEMON MUFFINS
WITH CHIA SEEDS

Preparation time 15 minutes • **Baking time** 20 minutes • **Makes** 12 muffins

Our lemon muffins are wonderfully fluffy and have a delightful crunch thanks to the chia seeds. The coconut sugar gives them a fantastic caramel flavor.

⅓ cup (80 ml) plus 1 tablespoon vegetable oil

½ vanilla bean

1 cup plus 1 tablespoon (130 g) spelt flour

1 cup (120 g) coconut flour

2 tablespoons black chia seeds

2 tablespoons white chia seeds

2 teaspoons baking powder

½ teaspoon baking soda

Pinch of salt

½ cup (100 g) coconut sugar

2 tablespoons grated lemon zest

2 tablespoons fresh lemon juice

1 cup (250 ml) almond milk

¾ cup plus 1 tablespoon (200 g) plain soy yogurt

SUGAR FREE

1 Preheat the oven to 400°F (200°C). Grease a twelve-cup muffin pan with 1 tablespoon of the vegetable oil.

2 Split the vanilla bean open lengthwise and scrape out the seeds with a knife. Set aside the pod.

3 Whisk together the spelt flour, coconut flour, black and white chia seeds, baking powder, baking soda, and salt in a medium bowl. In a separate bowl, whisk together the coconut sugar, lemon zest and juice, almond milk, yogurt, and the remaining ⅓ cup (80 ml) vegetable oil. Pour the wet ingredients into the dry ingredients and mix until just combined and no lumps remain. Fill each muffin cup two thirds of the way with batter.

4 Bake for 20 minutes, or until a cake tester inserted into the center of a muffin comes out clean.

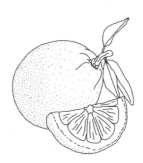

TIP

Instead of coconut sugar, you can use another sweetener. Raw or muscovado sugar also give a nice caramel flavor.

RAW CHOCOLATE TARTLETS

DEATH BY CHOCOLATE . . . BREAKFAST

Preparation time 15 minutes • **Soaking time** 8 hours • **Chilling time** 1 hour • **Makes** four 4-inch (10 cm) tartlets

It's finally okay to eat chocolate for breakfast! These tartlets may be decadent, but the healthy ingredients more than make up for the indulgence.

FOR THE FILLING

1½ cups (200 g) raw cashews

½ vanilla bean

⅓ cup (80 ml) maple syrup

3 tablespoons raw cacao powder

2 teaspoons fresh lemon juice

Pinch of salt

½ cup (100 ml) almond milk

1½ tablespoons solid coconut oil

FOR THE TARTLET BASE

1½ cups (220 g) raw almonds

3 tablespoons raw cacao powder

2 tablespoons maple syrup

2 tablespoons solid coconut oil

Pinch of salt

1 To make the filling, soak the cashews in water overnight (8 hours) in a covered container in the fridge.

2 In the morning, drain the cashews, rinse, and drain again.

3 Split the vanilla bean open lengthwise, and scrape out the seeds with a knife. Set aside the pod.

4 Place the cashews, vanilla seeds, maple syrup, cacao, lemon juice, salt, almond milk, and coconut oil in a food processor or high-speed blender and process until smooth. Pour into a piping bag (see Tip), place in the freezer, and chill for 30 minutes.

5 While the filling is chilling, make the base. Place the almonds, cacao, maple syrup, coconut oil, and salt in a food processor and pulse until well combined (it will be slightly sticky and smooth). Divide the mixture evenly between four 4-inch (10 cm) tartlet pans and press into the pans with your fingers. Refrigerate for at least 30 minutes.

6 Gently press the tartlet bases out of the pans and place on a plate. Pipe the filling into the bases. Chill until you're ready to serve.

TIPS

Our raw chocolate tartlets are best served with fresh berries, and a sprig of fresh mint, which balances the rich cake with brighter flavors.

If you don't have a piping bag, use a ziplock bag with a hole snipped in a corner.

WEEKEND BRUNCH